BUILDING PROFESSIONALS

CREATING A SUCCESSFUL PORTFOLIO

Dianne J. Orton

UNIVERSITY OF MISSOURI–COLUMBIA

Tammy L.W. Freelin

UNIVERSITY OF MISSOURI–COLUMBIA

Fresa J. Jacobs

UNIVERSITY OF MISSOURI–COLUMBIA

Robin R. Wingo

MINNESOTA STATE UNIVERSITY, MANKATO

Prentice
Hall

Upper Saddle River, New Jersey

Columbus, Ohio

D0472466

Vice President and Publisher: Jeffery W. Johnston
Senior Acquisitions Editor: Sande Johnson
Assistant Editor: Cecilia Johnson
Production Editor: Holcomb Hathaway
Design Coordinator: Diane C. Lorenzo
Cover Designer: Jeff Vanik
Cover Art: Eyewire
Production Manager: Pamela D. Bennett
Director of Marketing: Ann Castel Davis
Director of Advertising: Kevin Flanagan
Marketing Manager: Christina Quadhamer

This book was set in Sabon by Aerocraft Charter Art Service. It was printed and bound by Banta Book Group. The cover was printed by Phoenix Color Corp.

Pearson Education Ltd.
Pearson Education Australia Pty. Limited
Pearson Education Singapore Pte. Ltd.
Pearson Education North Asia Ltd.
Pearson Education Canada, Ltd.
Pearson Educación de Mexico, S.A. de C.V.
Pearson Education–Japan
Pearson Education Malaysia Pte. Ltd.
Pearson Education, *Upper Saddle River, New Jersey*

10 9 8 7 6 5 4 3
ISBN 0-13-049314-7

CONTENTS

NOTE: Every effort has been made to provide accurate and current Internet information in this book. However, the Internet and information posted on it are constantly changing, so it is inevitable that some of the Internet addresses listed in this textbook will change.

PREFACE

Welcome to *Building Professionals: Creating a Successful Portfolio.* We have been involved in higher education in a variety of roles and functions but always with the interest of assisting students during their college experience to prepare for rewarding and productive careers. Although our initial interest was with social work students, it soon became clear to us from our work in general education that learning ways to achieve success is an interest of all students. That interest is the same whether students are studying to be biologists, artists, business leaders, or teachers.

Building a professional portfolio is the challenge of learning about yourself and recognizing what you have learned in terms of knowledge, skills, and values in relation to your chosen field, and then finding opportunities to use them in a career. The unique framework of this portfolio prompts you to demonstrate to others (employers, professors, graduate programs, and so on) what you have learned, accomplished, or produced. Areas such as critical thinking, leadership, initiative/follow-through, working effectively with others, and communication provide structure as users progress through the important components of portfolio development. Incorporated into each component in this book is the opportunity for mentor feedback and designing a blueprint for growth.

We hope this book will aid you in the process of discovery, recognition, and documentation of your accomplishments—whatever your chosen field.

ACKNOWLEDGMENTS

The authors would like to thank Tara Collier, MSW, and Jeanne Link, MSW, for their contributions; Clark Johnson, Minnesota State University, for his comments and suggestions; and University of Missouri–Columbia field staff and students for trying out the reiterations of the Linking and Learning Worksheets. We would also like to thank our families, friends, and colleagues for their support.

Dianne J. Orton has been the Field Practicum coordinator at the School of Social Work, University of Missouri–Columbia, since 1991. Dianne received her Master of Social Work and Master of Arts in recreation therapy at the University of Iowa and earned her undergraduate degree in special education at the University of Northern Colorado. Dianne's career has included social work positions in the medical, child welfare, and school social work arenas. She has also been a special education teacher (K–12) and a higher education administrator in student services at a private institution.

At MU, Dianne is responsible for the management of both the undergraduate and graduate field education programs. She is also an advisor to undergraduate students and teaches field-related courses. Dianne's academic interests include teaching students journal-writing techniques during their field practicum experience that emphasize reflection, critical thinking, and problem-solving skills, and visual imagery that integrates photography and descriptive writing during students' capstone experience.

Tammy L. W. Freelin has served as the Coordinator for Student Services for the University of Missouri–Columbia School of Social Work since 1998. She received her MSW from the University of Missouri–Columbia with an emphasis in planning and administration and earned an undergraduate degree from the same institution in educational and counseling psychology.

Tammy's career has included case management, volunteer training and coordination, community organizing, and parenting education. At MU, Tammy is responsible for advising undergraduate and graduate students and student groups, coordinating admissions and recruitment, and advising on career-related issues.

Tresa J. Jacobs has worked at the School of Social Work, University of Missouri–Columbia, since 1998. She earned a BA in fine art with an emphasis in drawing from the University of Missouri in December of 2000. She also earned a BS in accounting from

Truman State University in 1997. Fresa's career has included a variety of experience, from layout and graphic design to database management and accounts payable. She has played Ultimate Frisbee in Columbia, Missouri, for the past four years.

Robin R. Wingo joined the faculty of the University of Missouri–Columbia in 1994, where she received her MSW with an emphasis in children and family. Her master's thesis focused on programs for juvenile delinquents who were committed to the state system for care and treatment.

Robin worked throughout the state of Missouri in a variety of treatment, consultant, training, and management capacities for over 20 years. Her earliest exposure to social service work was with adults who were chronically and persistently mentally ill. Following that, Robin worked with youth in residential care due to law violations and, as a social worker, worked with their families as the youth were released back into the community. She has also done pediatric, endocrinology, OB/GYN, and family practice social work in a Level I trauma and teaching hospital. Robin was involved in creating and coordinating the first statewide parenting "warm line" that provides support, research-based information, and referral to parents and professionals in Missouri. Robin has taught in both the undergraduate and graduate programs at the University of Missouri–Columbia and is currently teaching at Minnesota State University, Mankato.

Robin's teaching interests are practice methods and skills, practicum, and children/youth/family issues. She has also participated annually since 1999 in the Bristol (University) International Credit Earning Programme that focuses on comparative social policy.

What is a "portfolio" and why is it important? Webster's Dictionary defines *portfolio* simply as a "collection." We know that many professionals collect portfolios of their work. Artists, architects, designers, writers, and others all use a portfolio to demonstrate their competence and creativity in their chosen fields. Anyone can benefit from collecting evidence of abilities and pieces of professional work. This collection (or portfolio) can demonstrate to potential employers one's skills and abilities or may be part of an application for advanced training or graduate education. In addition, it can function as a professional development diary or journal.

We suggest that you use *Building Professionals* as a tool to document your professional progress. As your portfolio grows and you add more and more pieces of your professional work, you will find it quite useful throughout the job-search process. The portfolio you create can help you discover your abilities in relation to a desired position. It can also assist you in creating a resume and cover letter that accurately express your qualifications for an advertised position. An employer may not ask to see your portfolio, but bringing your portfolio with you to interviews may help you recount your skills and experiences to the interviewer.

Employers are looking for candidates who have a variety of skills. Knowing the body of work for your field is no longer enough to secure a job. The portfolio is designed to help you think critically about your skills and can indicate areas of growth. Employers look for a variety of qualities in potential employees, including those that appear in the following list of desirable employee traits. You will find it helpful to refer to this list as you build your portfolio.

Ability to run meetings

Analysis

Attention to detail

Civic responsibility

Collaboration

Confidence

Creativity

Critical thinking

Cultural competence

Diversity sensitivity

Effective writing skills

Ethical decision making

Financial management

Flexibility

Goal setting

International travel

Interpersonal communication

Knowledge of bureaucracy

Negotiation

Personal & professional balance

Personal initiative

Planning & organizational skills

Presentational skills

Prior work experience

Problem-solving capabilities

Professional image

Public speaking

Quick thinking

Sense of humor

Teamwork

Technology competencies

Time management

Understanding of company expectations

Procter and Gamble grouped these qualities into the following five categories. We use these categories throughout this book as a way to guide your thinking about your professional development.

CRITICAL THINKING AND PROBLEM SOLVING

- Demonstrates sound reasoning ability
- Analyzes complex data and identifies key issues
- Effectively combines analytical skill and intuition
- Learns from previous experiences and applies learning
- Handles give-and-take well

LEADERSHIP

- Creates a vision of what can be achieved
- Engages others in the vision
- Challenges self and inspires others to achieve the vision

INITIATIVE AND FOLLOW-THROUGH

- Identifies opportunities
- Sets challenging objectives
- Overcomes barriers to achieve objectives
- Keeps commitments
- Is a self-starter

WORKING EFFECTIVELY WITH OTHERS/DIVERSITY

- Has integrity and high personal standards
- Builds and maintains productive relationships
- Gets things done through and with others
- Is a team player

COMMUNICATION

- Expresses self clearly in verbal communication
- Expresses differing points of view without undermining others
- Expresses self clearly in written communication
- Demonstrates the ability to listen

When you reach Unit 7 of this book, you'll encounter the Linking and Learning Model. Visit **www.prenhall.com/orton** to download a copy of the Linking and Learning worksheet.

We suggest you begin your portfolio by developing your *personal statement or philosophy*. Personality inventories and self-assessments are a great way to learn more about yourself and your preferences. Many such assessments are available at campus career centers and on-line. Take some time to explore what is available to you.

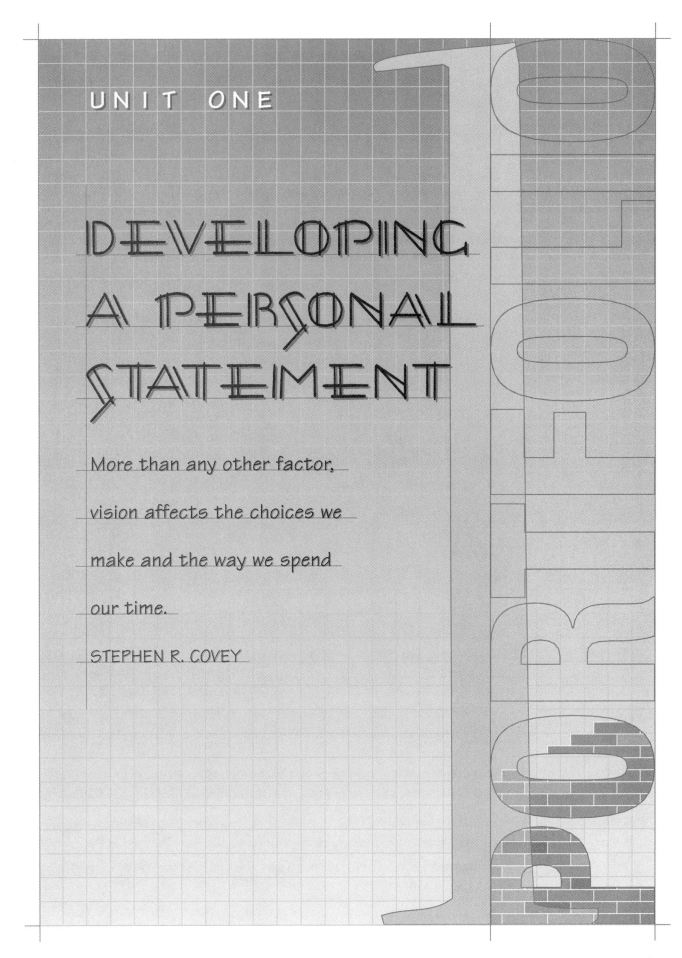

UNIT ONE

DEVELOPING A PERSONAL STATEMENT

More than any other factor,

vision affects the choices we

make and the way we spend

our time.

STEPHEN R. COVEY

Writing a personal statement for admission into graduate studies or professional schools, or to include with your resume when applying for jobs can be frustrating. It takes time to compose and revise your statement to create a focused, succinct, and well-written document. However, don't get discouraged—the process will ultimately be a rewarding experience.

Personal statements provide potential graduate and professional programs and employers an introduction of who you are as a person. Do not underestimate the importance of a personal statement as it provides a direct reflection of your values, educational goals, life/career goals, and character.

A few tips to consider when writing your personal statement:

- A well-written opening paragraph is important as it will be the blueprint for the remainder of the statement.
- Use positive language that has energy.
- Organize your statement so it flows from your worksheets.
- Personalize your statement so readers learn more about who you are.
- Check for and fix spelling and grammar mistakes.
- Gain insight into your learning style, personality, and aptitudes to help identify your strengths.

You may have already completed any number of personality, aptitude, or learning style inventories when you were first deciding on a college major. You might have also completed such inventories when applying for jobs. While such measures can never fully describe any individual and that person's unique characteristics, they can be valuable in highlighting some aspects not clearly identified previously. It is also true that people and personalities change over time with added maturity and experience. For this reason, we suggest that you revisit these measures and others as a first step to developing your professional portfolio.

Your local college career center will have a number of resources to help you develop your personal statement. You may also find the Student Success Supersite, www.prenhall.com/success/, to be helpful. In addition to these resources, we list below resources that you can find in bookstores, libraries, and on the Internet for additional ideas and insight.

Asher, Donald. (2000). *Graduate Admissions Essays: Write Your Way into the Graduate School of Your Choice.* Ten Speed Press.

Baron, Renee. (1998). *What Type Am I?: Discover Who You Really Are.* Penguin USA.

Covey, Stephen R. (1990). *The Seven Habits of Highly Effective People.* Franklin Covey.

Jones, Laurie Beth. (1996). *The Path: Creating Your Mission Statement for Work and Life.* Hyperion.

Keirsey Temperament Sorter II. www.advisorteam.com.

Learning Styles Questionnaire. www2.ncsu.edu/unity/lockers/users/f/felder/public/ILSdir/ilsweb.html

Maslow, Abraham. (1970). *Motivation and Personality,* 2nd Ed. Harper & Row.

Mason, Michael James. (2000). *How to Write a Winning College Application Essay.* Prima Publishing.

Richardson, John. (2000). *Mastering the Personal Statement.* Richardson Press.

Stelzer, Richard. (1997). *How to Write a Personal Statement for Graduate and Professional School.* Peterson's Guides.

Type Focus™ (free personality inventory). www.typefocus.com.

We do not envision the "personal statement" you develop here as a rigid sentence or essay. Rather, you may wish to use this as a place to jot down some common themes that emerge from your personal research. You may also wish to include the results of some of your inventories in this section for later reference. The foundation created by a personal statement will provide direction, insight, and additional avenues for exploration as your professional portfolio is constructed.

PERSONAL STATEMENT

Social work is not only a profession—it is also a commitment to social change, to client empowerment, and to addressing difficult and challenging issues that individuals, families, and communities face. As a social worker, I face daily professional and personal trials and challenges, and I must have a firm foundation on which to base my practice.

As I have learned through graduate studies and work experience, it is very important to have effective interaction and communication skills when working with clients and their families. It is also crucial to be organized and responsible, and to manage time well. I am continuing to learn to respond empathetically to clients, and I try to place myself in clients' shoes to truly understand their needs, values, and goals.

It is beneficial for me as a social worker to be a team player, and to work on developing my communication skills, both written and verbal. I must be able to accept constructive criticism and be open to suggestions from others regarding how to do things more effectively and efficiently. I am also learning about the importance of advocating for clients, and I am becoming more confident and assertive when clients need someone to speak on their behalf.

One of the most important assets of a social worker is the ability to apply the concept of the Strengths Perspective and the Person-In-Environment Theory. I am learning to focus on a client's strengths and abilities, instead of their weaknesses and limitations. It is important to not focus only on one area of a client's life, but to look at the whole person—their family life, past experiences, and environment—using the concept of circular causality. Empowering clients is one of social workers' greatest opportunities; I want clients to realize that I, as the social worker, merely pump the gas into the car—the client does the driving. Through experience, I am learning to be resourceful, to problem solve creatively, and to understand the importance of developing networking and brokering skills. Also, I am learning that flexibility and accountability are crucial qualities in a social worker in order to work successfully for and with clients.

Setting boundaries is another important aspect of social work; unfortunately this is extremely difficult to learn to do. Getting enough rest, eating properly, and setting time limits—taking care of myself—allows me to remain healthy and to work more effectively with clients and other professionals.

Finally, as a social worker it is important to never stop growing professionally or personally. Ongoing education through attending workshops, reading journals, and participating in self and agency evaluations is necessary in order for me to grow as a professional and for social work to grow as a profession.

CRITICAL THINKING AND PROBLEM SOLVING

As a case manager for children and adults with developmental disabilities, I learned how to assess clients presenting problems and how to help empower clients in identifying their needs and seting goals for the future.

LEADERSHIP

During high school and college I often took on leadership roles in clubs and organizations. Now, as a professional, I am often relied upon as a facilitator during interagency meetings. I have also been given leadership responsibilities in the workplace, such as being asked to help develop a juvenile drug and alcohol recovery program.

INITIATIVE AND FOLLOW THROUGH

I often approach my supervisors and ask them to identify for me areas of possible professional growth and improvement. Employers appreciate staff who are willing to identify these areas and who work on becoming more effective in the workplace.

WORKING EFFECTIVELY WITH OTHERS/DIVERSITY

A team player means choosing to not gossip and respecting others' values, priorities, and beliefs. I also look for opportunities to attend workshops that address issues and populations about which I lack knowledge. I also enjoy volunteering on the social committees where I work.

COMMUNICATION

I have often been complimented on my writing abilities. I would like to develop my verbal communication skills, and to do that I have had to step out of my comfort zone. During a graduate research assistantship, I volunteered to interview clients with drug and alcohol addictions over the phone and in person in a corrections setting. Networking with other agencies has helped me to build my knowledge base and pool of resources, which has increased my effectiveness when working with clients.

PERSONAL ACHIEVEMENT
ROUGH DRAFT

Critical Thinking and Problem Solving

Leadership

Initiative and Follow-Through

Working Effectively with Others

Communication

PERSONAL ACHIEVEMENT
BLUEPRINTS

Strengths in this Area:

Areas for Growth:

Blueprint for Improvement:

Reviews, Updates, Advisor Comments:

PERSONAL ACHIEVEMENT
ROUGH DRAFT

Critical Thinking and Problem Solving

Leadership

Initiative and Follow-Through

Working Effectively with Others

Communication

PERSONAL ACHIEVEMENT
BLUEPRINTS

Strengths in this Area:

Areas for Growth:

Blueprint for Improvement:

Reviews, Updates, Advisor Comments:

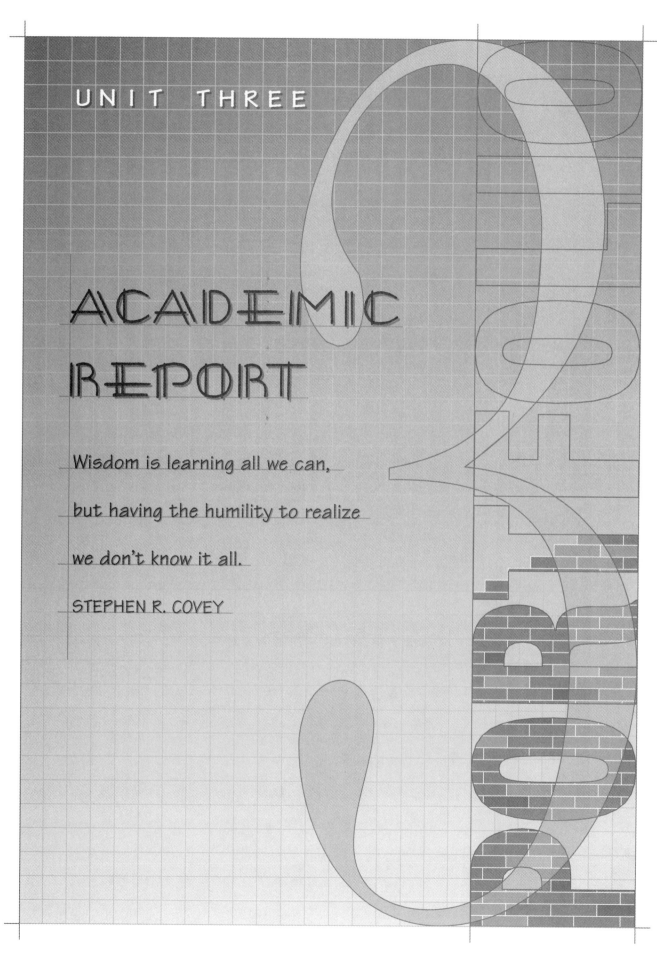

UNIT THREE

ACADEMIC REPORT

Wisdom is learning all we can,

but having the humility to realize

we don't know it all.

STEPHEN R. COVEY

We recommend you include examples of the following in the **Acadmic Report** section of your portfolio.

- Transcripts
- Course descriptions
- Syllabi
- Sample papers
- Sample work

1. Gather information on your undergraduate education, including transcripts, descriptions of courses, syllabi, sample research papers, and any other work.

    a. Did your area of concentration include any notable classes?

    b. Were you recognized or given awards for your GPA?

    c. Have you received any honors or published papers?

2. Think about how the above information outlines your academic success.

    a. Do you notice any particular areas that could be listed as strengths?

    b. Do you find your writing or any other area could be seen as a strength?

    c. Explain any volunteer experiences that were relevant to your concentration.

Use the following examples as a springboard for ideas for your worksheet.

CRITICAL THINKING AND PROBLEM SOLVING

Engaged in policy-making decisions and strategic thinking on the board of Kappa Omicron Nu honor society board of directors.

LEADERSHIP

President of the Chi Delta chapter of the Phi Alpha honor society.

INITIATIVE AND FOLLOW-THROUGH

I took my research papers to the editor of one of the school's weekly publications for feedback on my writing style.

WORKING EFFECTIVELY WITH OTHERS

I served as an intern to the staff at church, and also worked with youth and children as a peer counselor.

COMMUNICATION

Several of my professors have made comments on my academic improvement and willingness to sharpen the areas that needed improvement.

ACADEMIC REPORT

Critical Thinking and Problem Solving

Leadership

Initiative and Follow-Through

Working Effectively with Others

Communication

ACADEMIC REPORT
B L U E P R I N T S

Strengths in this Area:

Areas for Growth:

Blueprint for Improvement:

Reviews, Updates, Advisor Comments:

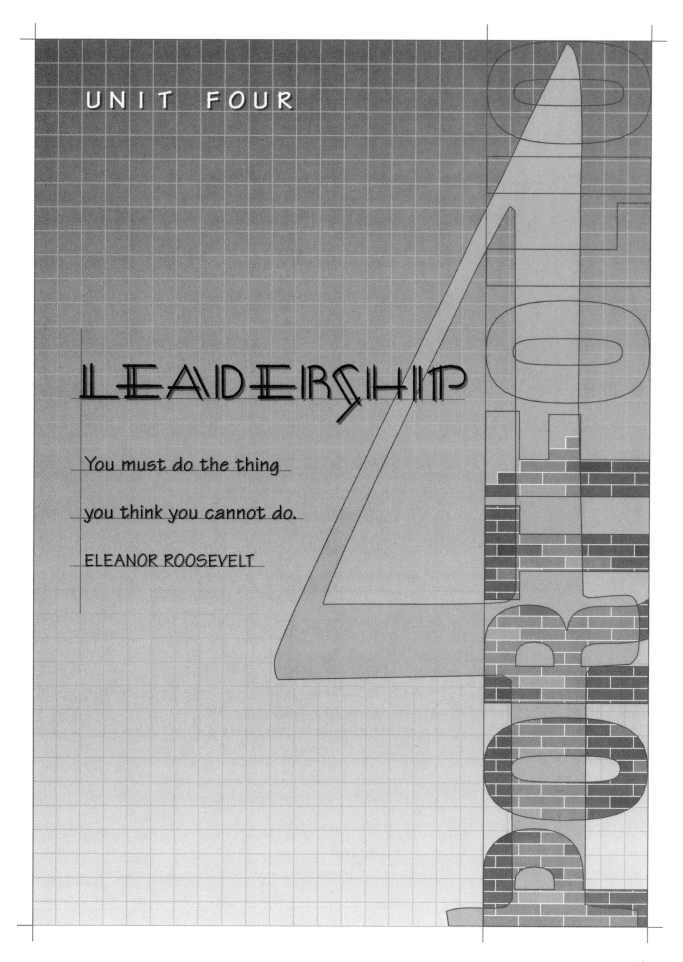

UNIT FOUR

LEADERSHIP

You must do the thing

you think you cannot do.

ELEANOR ROOSEVELT

We recommend you include examples of the following in the **Leadership** section of your portfolio.

- Student services
- Student government
- Activities on campus
- Activities in the community
- Board committees
- Advisory groups
- Group membership

1. Compile a list of student services, student government, and any campus or community activities in which you have been involved.

   a. Do any of these efforts pertain to the area of employment you seek or graduate school curriculum to which you are applying?

   b. Have you received any awards surrounding your work as a leader?

   c. Is there any relevant volunteer experience that highlights your leadership skills?

2. Think about how the above information describes you as a leader.

   a. Do you notice any weaknesses or areas that need improvement?

   b. What areas do you feel you may have missed or would need additional work?

   Use the following examples as a springboard for ideas for your worksheet.

CRITICAL THINKING AND PROBLEM SOLVING

During my internship my supervisor complimented me on my problem-solving skills in dealing with finding housing for a family.

LEADERSHIP

Member of the School of Social Work search committee, helped to interview new faculty for vacant spots.

INITIATIVE AND FOLLOW-THROUGH

While working as an activities assistant at the local care center I created and organized various client activities.

WORKING EFFECTIVELY WITH OTHERS

Involved as a group facilitator for the Division of Family Services and developed outstanding people skills and cultural sensitivity.

COMMUNICATION

Honors Ambassador: acted as a liaison between the students and the director of the Honors College. Met with prospective students to discuss resources.

Critical Thinking and Problem Solving

Leadership

Initiative and Follow-Through

Working Effectively with Others

Communication

LEADERSHIP
BLUEPRINTS

Strengths in this Area:

Areas for Growth:

Blueprint for Improvement:

Reviews, Updates, Advisor Comments:

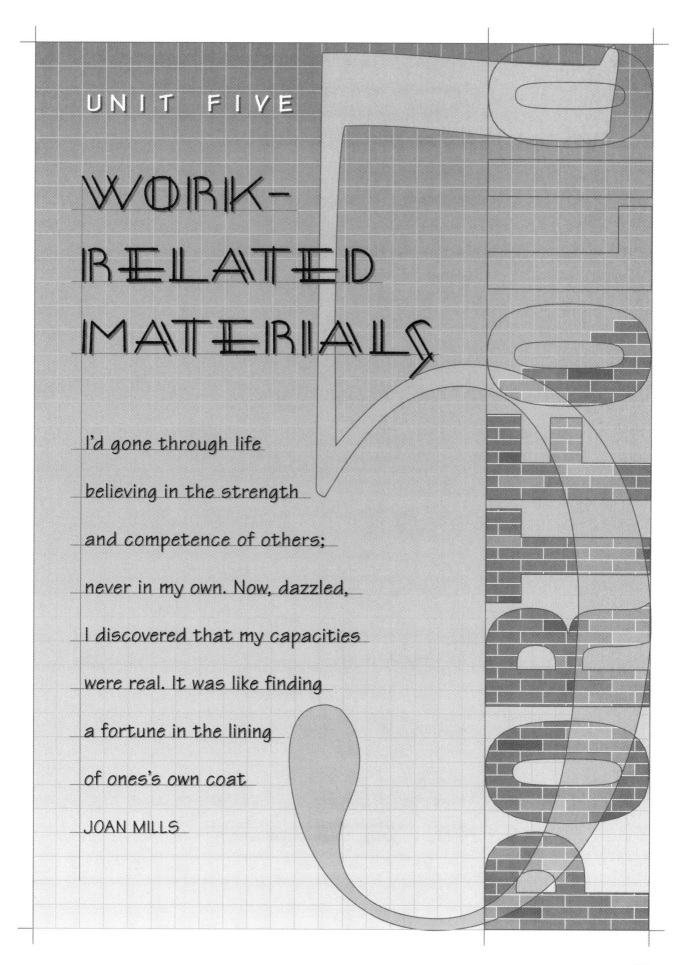

WORK-RELATED MATERIALS

I'd gone through life

believing in the strength

and competence of others;

never in my own. Now, dazzled,

I discovered that my capacities

were real. It was like finding

a fortune in the lining

of ones's own coat

JOAN MILLS

We recommend you include examples of the following in the **Work-Related** section of your portfolio.

- Job descriptions
- Evaluations
- Teaching assistantships
- Research assistantships
- Consultation

1. Gather all relevant information pertaining to job descriptions, assistantships, and evaluations.
   a. Do you have relevant work experience that stands out for you or would interest prospective employers?
   b. Have you any examples of highly satisfactory evaluations?
   c. Have employers recognized abilities you possess?

2. How does the above information describe you as a person?
   a. Do you notice specific strengths?
   b. What areas on the evaluation do you feel need improvement?
   c. Are there any areas that you sought to explore outside of jobs or assistantships?

Use the following examples as a springboard for ideas for your worksheet.

CRITICAL THINKING AND PROBLEM SOLVING

At my last position with the Division of Family Services, I created a needs assessment to address the growing population of immigrants coming into our town. My supervisor and I recognized the need and I helped to identify the areas of concern.

LEADERSHIP

Participated as Student Board Member, engaged in policy-making decisions and strategic planning for Kappa Omicron Nu.

INITIATIVE AND FOLLOW-THROUGH

During an assistantship I created various activities and services in the area of art therapy.

WORKING EFFECTIVELY WITH OTHERS

Worked with students to raise awareness of the Hispanic culture.

COMMUNICATION

Communicated weekly with supervisor regarding my progress during my internship. This made my experience more of a learning experience and allowed me to monitor my own progress.

WORK-RELATED
ROUGH DRAFT

Critical Thinking and Problem Solving

Leadership

Initiative and Follow-Through

Working Effectively with Others

Communication

WORK-RELATED
BLUEPRINTS

Strengths in this Area:

Areas for Growth:

Blueprint for Improvement:

Reviews, Updates, Advisor Comments:

UNIT SIX

INTERNSHIPS

In the world there are

different and still more

different people. Sit

and mix with everyone,

the way a boat joins

the river.

TULSIDAS

We recommend you include examples of the following in the **Internships** section of your portfolio.

- Learning plan
- Linking & Learning Worksheets*
- Project samples
- Evaluation

Linking & Learning Worksheets are explained in the following section.

1. Gather examples of Linking & Learning Worksheets, project samples, and learning plans completed from any previous internship.

   a. In completing your Linking & Learning Worksheets did you notice any ethical dilemmas that sparked your thinking?

   b. What problems did you run into in completing your lesson plan?

   c. What project did you complete that stemmed from undergraduate course work?

2. Think about how all the above information has shaped your learning.

   a. Do you notice any emerging theories used in your internship?

   b. List any specific strengths gathered from your experience.

   c. Can you see any "bad habits" you may have picked up?

Use the following examples as a springboard for ideas for your worksheet.

CRITICAL THINKING AND PROBLEM SOLVING

During my internship I recognized the problem the agency was having with staff morale and made suggestions that the director used during his restructuring.

LEADERSHIP

Was asked to sit on the board during my internship with Division of Family Services to help identify areas of quality assurance within the agency.

INITIATIVE AND FOLLOW-THROUGH

Took the initiative to structure my weekly meetings with my supervisor, who was not sure how meetings were to be conducted, so I could receive maximum input from the staff.

WORKING EFFECTIVELY WITH OTHERS

Work with staff of all cultural backgrounds to shape my internship experience.

COMMUNICATION

Kept the lines of communication open between the school and the agency to ensure a successful experience.

Used Linking & Learning Worksheets to ensure active communication between field instructor and student.

INTERNSHIPS
ROUGH DRAFT

Critical Thinking and Problem Solving

Leadership

Initiative and Follow-Through

Working Effectively with Others

Communication

INTERNSHIPS
B L U E P R I N T S

Strengths in this Area:

Areas for Growth:

Blueprint for Improvement:

Reviews, Updates, Advisor Comments:

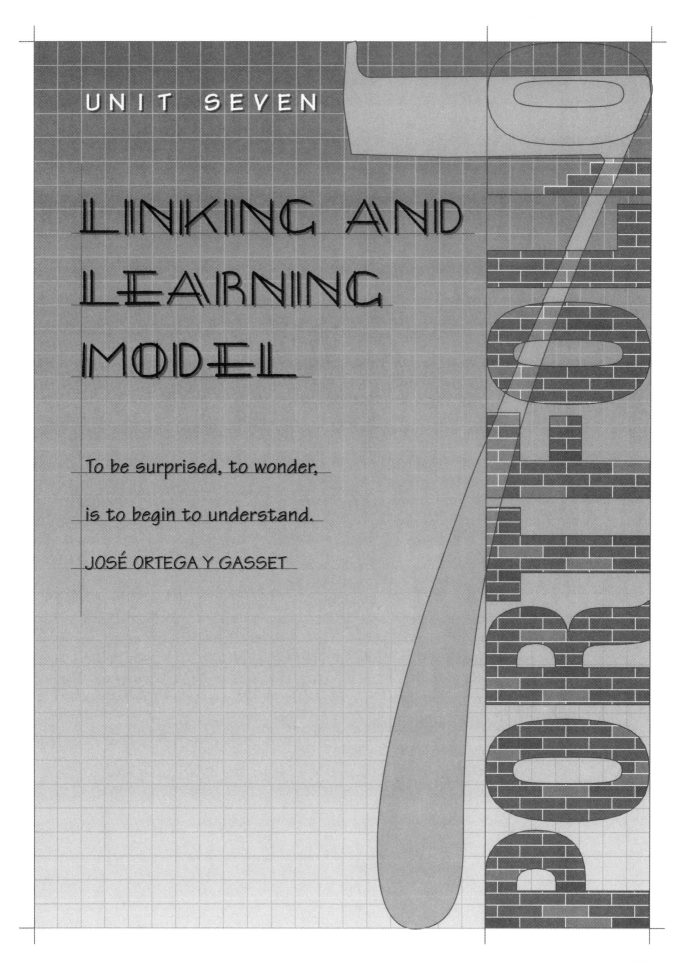

UNIT SEVEN

LINKING AND LEARNING MODEL

To be surprised, to wonder,

is to begin to understand.

JOSÉ ORTEGA Y GASSET

Most professional academic programs require applied course work that provides students the opportunity to integrate previous experience with classroom and current learning while carrying out a professional role within a structured learning environment. This may be in a social service agency, public school system, hospital/clinic, or business setting.

A major goal of applied courses, whether internships, student teaching, or clinical experience, is to facilitate, monitor, and assess students' learning goals, personal and professional strengths and limitations, development of critical-thinking/problem-solving abilities, and mastery of self-directed practice skills. Helping you create, monitor, and assess these goals is the purpose of the Linking and Learning Model.

Most internship, student teaching, and clinical settings require some method of accountability that is reviewed on a regular basis with a practice supervisor or mentor. The review is often shared with university and college faculty on a regular basis and can provide a structure and focus for weekly or biweekly supervisory meetings. The Linking and Learning Model is an evaluative method designed to enhance student learning through integration of classroom and applied knowledge. Evidence of that integration is often required to advance in professional programs.

The Linking and Learning Model embraces professional programs with a format that allows students to respond to learning objectives and goals that are specific to their discipline. While individual professions may have their own specific theories, techniques, models, and skills for student learning, the Linking and Learning Model recognizes and provides the format to customize a model suitable to a variety of disciplines and settings. Visit **www.prenhall.com/orton** to download a copy of the Linking and Learning worksheet.

The format of the Linking and Learning Model is illustrated in the examples below. The *vertical axis* on the model is universal to all disciplines. It includes:

Course work, activities, learning plan objectives, etc.

Skills, theories, models, techniques identified and utilized.

Plan of action

Inquiry

Reflections

The *horizontal axis* responds to the issues, concerns, and learning assignments of specific disciplines. The horizontal axis could include headings such as the following, among many others:

Code of Ethics/Professional Behavior Standards

Content areas such as Lesson Plan, Financial Planning, Budgeting, Marketing Strategies, Research, or Evaluation

Ethical Dilemma/Problem-Solving Models

Days of the Week (less structured)

Educational/Therapy Group Sessions

Licensure Supervision Record

Continuing Education Workshops/Conference Documentation

Observation Report

CODE OF ETHICS

	Social Justice	Dignity & Worth	Integrity
Course Work, Activities, Learning Plan Objectives, etc.			
Skills, Theories, Models, Techniques Identified and Utilized			

LESSON PLAN

	Math	English	Social Studies
Course Work, Activities, Learning Plan Objectives, etc.			
Skills, Theories, Models, Techniques Identified and Utilized			

LINKING AND LEARNING MODEL EXAMPLE

	GOAL 1 To gain an understanding of the FEMA organizational structure	GOAL 2 To develop a knowledge base regarding the disaster mitigation programs administered by FEMA	GOAL 3 To observe the roles and relationships of diverse and varied FEMA personnel
COURSE WORK, ACTIVITIES, LEARNING PLAN OBJECTIVES, ETC. *Plan your work—work your plan!*	Determine the appropriate mechanisms for accomplishing tasks through the FEMA structure.	Seek opportunities to participate in community forums regarding mitigation programs.	Establish productive relationships with FEMA officials and other emergency management professionals.
SKILLS, THEORIES, MODELS, TECHNIQUES IDENTIFIED AND UTILIZED *You have to do a thing to learn to do it!*	Bureaucratic model. Hierarchical in nature.	Generalist practice.	Personality types distinguished by dominant need orientation (McClelland).
PLAN OF ACTION *There isn't any map for the road to success; you have to make your own!*	Focused on my general office responsibilities as a FEMA intern. These include participating in the process of obtaining travel authorization, vouchering, and utilizing the common mitigation calendar.	Attended a meeting of the City Council for the City of Hannibal, Missouri, during which the initial phases of Project Impact were adopted. Participated in Project Impact committee meeting in Neosho, Missouri.	Attended meetings with FEMA personnel around the state of Missouri. Had the opportunity to converse regarding diverse topics including ideas about the progression of projects and the frustrations of the bureaucracy.
AHA'S OR QUESTIONS *If you expand a person's mind, it never contracts to its original position!*	Being part of a large bureaucratic (systematic) agency requires employees to participate in the functions of the agency designed to facilitate the continuation of the organization. Although these functions sometimes seem to conflict with and complicate the service mission of the organization, they are ultimately necessary in certain forms.	For the purposes of my internship, it is more important to view the stages through which communities are moving in the Project Impact process, than to focus on the specific details of a particular community.	Developing professional relationships with colleagues allows for the sharing of ideas and thoughts regarding the administration of programs and possible avenues for improvement.

LINKING AND LEARNING MODEL EXAMPLE, continued

	GOAL 4	GOAL 5	GOAL 6
	To become proficient in FEMA terminology and procedures, specifically concerning disaster mitigation	To efficiently integrate social work ideals with FEMA protocol and procedures	To develop appropriate evaluation skills and processes regarding FEMA programs and objectives
COURSE WORK, ACTIVITIES, LEARNING PLAN OBJECTIVES, ETC. *Plan your work—work your plan!*	Utilize knowledge regarding mitigation terminology to develop an understanding of community experiences with programs.	Develop positive and productive contacts with community leaders interested in mitigation efforts.	Create evaluation mechanisms to assist in the evaluation of Project Impact methods.
SKILLS, THEORIES, MODELS, TECHNIQUES IDENTIFIED AND UTILIZED *You have to do a thing to learn to do it!*	Generalist practice.	Systems theory.	Process evaluation utilizing customer service components.
PLAN OF ACTION *There isn't any map for the road to success; you have to make your own!*	Participated in a meeting regarding the development of a disaster relevant group of displays sponsored by MEMC for the Kansas City area home show in March 2001.	Attended Project Impact committee meeting in Neosho, Missouri. At the meeting, one of the main topics for discussion included efforts regarding mitigation against school violence, which is a form of terrorism when perpetrated on these communities.	Developed questions for the process evaluation utilizing customer service survey principles. Discussed the requirements of a larger behavioral change study designed to evaluate the larger effects of Project Impact on communities and their citizens.
AHA'S OR QUESTIONS *If you expand a person's mind, it never contracts to its original position!*	Planning and developing the proper presentation of public education materials is nearly as important as the information provided by the materials. If the target population is not marketed to in a manner consistent with their knowledge and interest bases, then materials will be unusable to these individuals.	While listening to the discussion regarding efforts to retain a speaker who could educate parents, teachers, and students regarding school violence, I realized that mental health professionals, including social workers, were absent from the thought process. The inclusion of primarily emergency responders neglects the role social workers have before and after a crisis, and their abilities to help mitigate responses.	Writing questions for a survey can be extremely complicated. Determining the proper phrases and words that will provide the respondent with the clearest thoughts regarding the intent of the question is a matter for careful consideration. It merits saying again, "Garbage in, garbage out."

LINKING AND LEARNING MODEL EXAMPLE, continued

Pick one idea, issue, theory, AHA, question, event, etc. Write about it in more detail. Include your subjective as well as objective thoughts about the topic.

In order to clearly understand the manner in which Project Impact and other FEMA mitigation programs are designed to serve the members of their constituencies, I took the opportunity to review and evaluate policies and guidance procedures developed for these programs. Within these documents are their foundations, including the requirements established to ensure government monies will be used to further certain goals and objectives. However, once these programs begin to interface with the constituencies they are designed to serve, many areas and opportunities for maneuvering are brought to light.

Because I appreciate the need for freedom and the ability to mold a program or policy to meet the needs of its consumers, the opportunity for government officials to work with communities to implement programs in a manner consistent with the goals and objectives of all involved parties is well viewed. Conversations with fellow FEMA colleagues and members of Project Impact communities have shown me the importance of intergovernmental cooperation. The only minor concern is the level of compromise that may sometimes be necessary to develop a plan or project that all involved parties will be committed to.

After contemplating the pros and cons of maneuverability, I believe that the ability for government programs to be flexible in the delivery of services allows for better use of taxpayer monies by allowing for the investment of local constituencies in projects that affect their lives on a daily and continuing basis. Thus, efforts to stifle the ability of communities to meet their needs through the legal maneuvering of certain policies and procedures should be controlled.

	Signature & Date	Comments
Student		
Supervisor		

TIME LOG							
Week of:	Monday	Tuesday	Wednesday	Thursday	Friday	Sat/Sun	Total

Created by Dianne Orton & Robin Wingo 2001

LINKING AND LEARNING WORKSHEET

	GOAL 1	GOAL 2	GOAL 3	GOAL 4
COURSE WORK, ACTIVITIES, LEARNING PLAN OBJECTIVES, ETC. *Plan your work—work your plan!*				
SKILLS, THEORIES, MODELS, TECHNIQUES IDENTIFIED AND UTILIZED *You have to do a thing to learn to do it!*				
PLAN OF ACTION *There isn't any map for the road to success; you have to make your own!*				
AHA'S OR QUESTIONS *If you expand a person's mind, it never contracts to its original position!*				

LINKING AND LEARNING MODEL WORKSHEET

Pick one idea, issue, theory, aha, question, event, etc. Write about it in more detail. Include your subjective as well as objective thoughts about the topic.

	Signature & Date	Comments
Student		
Supervisor		

TIME LOG							
Week of:	Monday	Tuesday	Wednesday	Thursday	Friday	Sat/Sun	Total

Created by Dianne Orton & Robin Wingo 2001

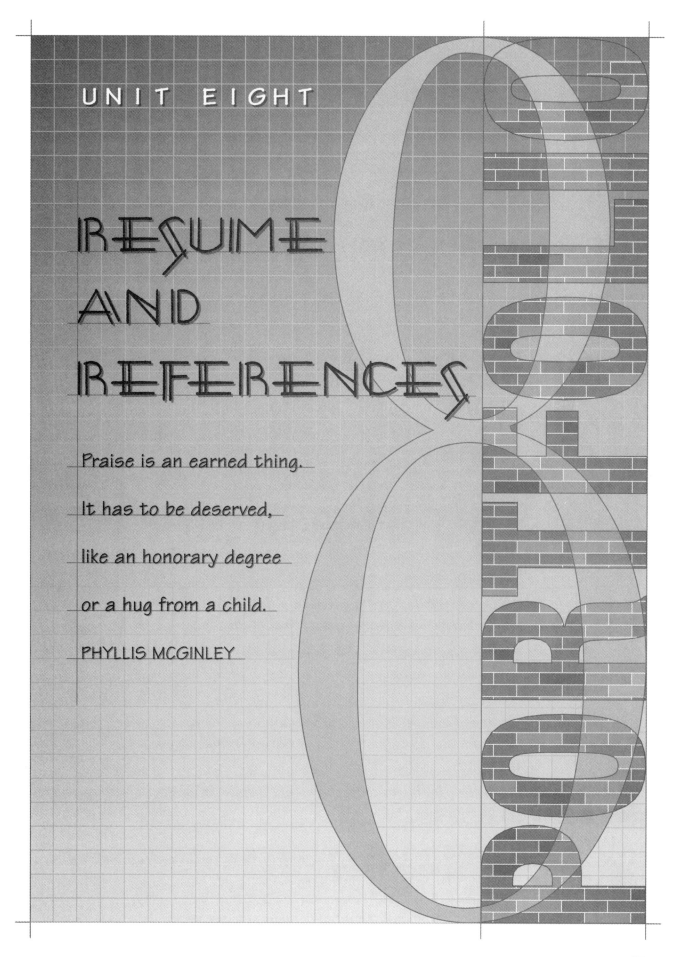

UNIT EIGHT

RESUME AND REFERENCES

Praise is an earned thing.

It has to be deserved,

like an honorary degree

or a hug from a child.

PHYLLIS MCGINLEY

We recommend you include examples of the following in the **Resume and References** section of your portfolio.

- Cover letter
- Letters of reference
- Resume

1. Gather information from the other sections of this portfolio and summarize in this section. This is a great way to organize the information recorded in this portfolio. Use this information as a blueprint for creating your cover letter and resume.

2. Think about how this information fits together in the construction of your resume.

   a. Is there a common theme?

   b. What are your strengths?

   c. Are there areas that need improvement?

   d. For what kinds of employment opportunities are you looking?

   Use the following example as a springboard for organizing your own information.

CRITICAL THINKING AND PROBLEM SOLVING

Personal Achievements: Supervisor at the animal shelter complimented me on my creative advertising idea.

Academic Report: Engaged in policy-making decisions on the Kappa Omicron Nu honor society board of directors.

Leadership: My supervisor complimented me on my problem-solving skills in dealing with finding housing for a family.

Work-Related: Created a needs assessment to address the growing population of immigrants coming into our town. We recognized the need, and I helped to identify the areas of concern.

Internships: During my internship, I recognized that the agency was having problems with staff morale and the director used my suggestions during restructuring.

LEADERSHIP

Personal Achievements: Participated in student government in high school and organized activities for my dorm.

Academic Report: President of the Chi Delta chapter of the Phi Alpha honors society two semesters in a row.

Leadership: Member of School Search committee, helped to interview new faculty for vacant positions.

Work-Related: Participated as a Student Board Member, engaged in policy-making decisions and strategic planning for Kappa Omicron Nu.

Internships: Was asked to sit on the board during my internship to help identify areas of quality assurance within the agency.

INITIATIVE AND FOLLOW-THROUGH

Personal Achievements: I helped my supervisor at the animal shelter work on the advertising idea I proposed.

Academic Report: Took research papers to editor of school's weekly publication for feedback on my writing style.

Leadership: Created and organized various client activities while working at local care center.

Work-Related: During an assistantship I created various activities and services in the area of art therapy.

Internships: Took the initiative to structure my weekly meetings, so I could receive maximum input from staff.

WORKING EFFECTIVELY WITH OTHERS/DIVERSITY

Personal Achievements: I am the designated Welcome Wagon representative for my dorm.

Academic Report: Served as an intern to the staff at church. Worked with youth and children as a peer counselor.

Leadership: Involved as a group facilitator for the Division of Family Services, developed outstanding people skills and cultural sensitivity.

Work-Related: Worked with social work students to raise awareness of the Hispanic culture.

Internships: Worked with staff of all cultural backgrounds to shape my internship experience.

COMMUNICATION

Personal Achievements: My professor commented on how my writing has improved since last semester. I'm enjoying my papers more now.

Academic Report: Several of my professors have made comments on my academic improvement and willingness to sharpen the areas that needed improvement.

Leadership: Honors Ambassador– liaison between students and director of the honors college. Met with prospective students to discuss resources.

Work-Related: Communicated weekly with supervisor regarding my progress during my internship.

Internships: Kept the lines of communication open between the school and the agency to ensure a successful experience.

RESUME AND REFERENCES
BLUEPRINTS

Critical Thinking and Problem Solving

Leadership

Initiative and Follow-Through

Working Effectively with Others

Communication

Sample Cover Letter

October 12, 2002

Ms. Evelyn Smith
Missouri Division of Family Services
211 E. Grand Avenue
St. Louis, MO 63001

Dear Ms. Smith,

While attending a DFS seminar in St. Louis last week, I learned that your agency might be hiring an additional caseworker to assist with child abuse and neglect. I am writing to inquire further about this potential position.

I am currently enrolled as a School of Social Work student at the University of Missouri in Columbia. Although I do not anticipate graduation until May 2003, I feel that my current creative and technical skills, as well as my interest in the area of child abuse and neglect, would qualify me to do the type of work you require. As outlined on my enclosed resume, I have had experience with the Division of Family Services. In addition, I place a high priority on consumer confidentiality and teamwork, qualities that would make me a valuable addition to your agency.

I am impressed by the reputation of your agency and feel confident that my qualifications would enable me to perform the job well. I am excited about the opportunity for growth and learning afforded me by working with your team. I would appreciate an opportunity to meet with you and discuss my qualifications and to learn more about this job. I will call you the week of November 6 to see if a meeting can be arranged. In the meantime, I may be reached at (573) 555-5555.

Thanks for you consideration. I look forward to meeting with you.

Sincerely yours,

Jane T. Doe

Jane T. Doe

Enclosure

Sample Resume

JANE T. DOE

555 Capital Drive, Columbia, Missouri 65203   573-555-5555 e-mail: JaneDoe@mizzou.edu

EDUCATION

University of Missouri   *M.S.W. in Social Work, 3.8/4.0 GPA, August 2001 to May 2003*
Area of Concentration: Children and Family Services

Columbia College   *B.A. in Psychology, 4.0/4.0 GPA, August 1998 to May 2001*

WORK EXPERIENCE

Social Work Intern, *Division of Family Services, Columbia, Missouri*
May 2002 to August 2002

- Worked with children and families during times of crisis by providing stability to children while placed in emergency out-of-home care, and provided follow-up support services to families once the placement ended.
- Worked on board to help identify areas of quality assurance within the agency.
- Performed a number of duties including psychosocial assessments, home visits, and individual work with children, and participated in community-wide parent education planning.

Residential Specialist, *Burrell-Bramblewood Group Home, Nixa, Missouri*
May 2001 to May 2002

- Provided care and emotional support to children in a psychiatric group home. Assisted the director with various duties.

Volunteer, *The Animal Shelter, Columbia, MO*
June 1994 to May 1996

- Contributed and worked on shelter's advertising campaign.

RELATED PROFESSIONAL INFORMATION

School of Social Work Search Committee, *January 2003 to May 2003.*
Helped interview new faculty for vacant spots

Kappa Omicron Nu, *December 1999 to May 2003*
Honor Society
Engaged in policy-making decisions on Board of Directors

Phi Alpha, *December 2001 to May 2003*
Social Work Honor Society
President of chapter for two semesters

Who's Who Among Students In America's Colleges and Universities, *October 1998 to May 2001*
Honored as one of 99 students at Columbia College to receive this award for above-average academic standing, community service, leadership ability, and potential for continued success.

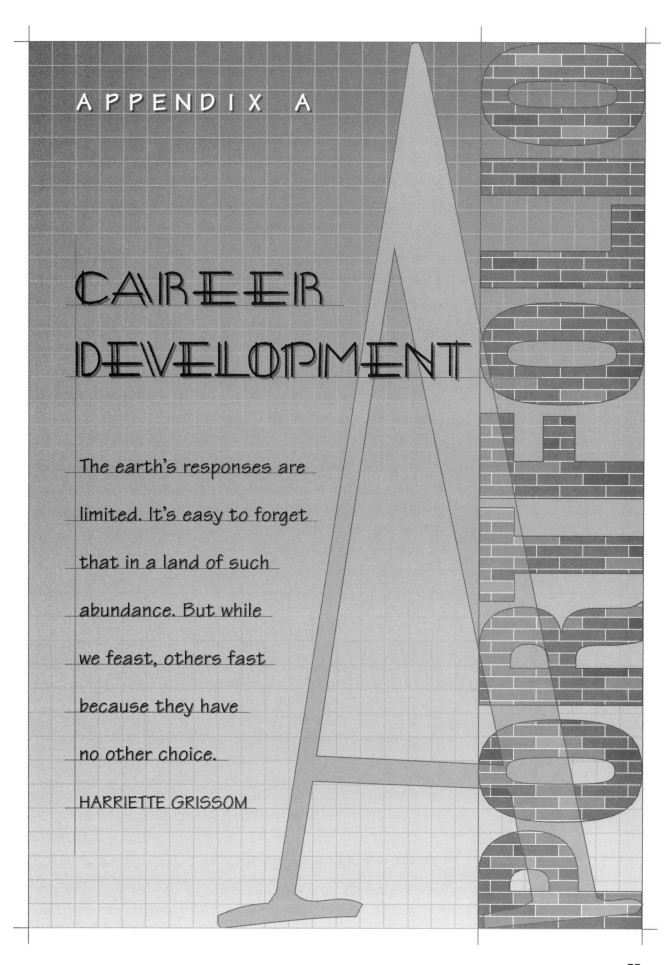

APPENDIX A

CAREER DEVELOPMENT

The earth's responses are

limited. It's easy to forget

that in a land of such

abundance. But while

we feast, others fast

because they have

no other choice.

HARRIETTE GRISSOM

The process of applying for jobs in your chosen field can be intensive, challenging, and time consuming. As you complete applications and prepare for interviews, think about the analysis of your undergraduate work you performed while using this portfolio guide. You have already identified some of the key elements employers look for:

- Critical thinking and problem solving
- Leadership
- Initiative and follow-through
- Working effectively with others/diversity
- Communication.

The following are suggestions for integrating your portfolio development work into your job search:

- As you develop your portfolio, edit and format it in a professional manner to ensure it will always be ready for presentation at an interview or job fair.
- Develop an abbreviated version of your portfolio to leave with prospective employers at job fairs or at open call interviews. The abbreviated version should include your personal statement, an overview of your achievements, and an outline of your key projects integrating the five categories.
- Make your targeted job site aware that you have a portfolio that they can examine when you interview.
- Consider taking a copy of your complete portfolio with you to leave with the interviewer. This may be a greater investment than you can routinely afford, but for those positions you feel strongly are a good fit for your skills and abilities, you may want to consider it an investment. The interviewer may see it the same way.
- We suggest that you include not only unmarked final drafts in your portfolio but also any work that demonstrates project development, writing samples, collaboration skills, and use of process over time. These will help your interviewer judge your abilities to integrate feedback, to learn, and to work as a team member.

ADDITIONAL RESOURCES

As you use this guide to examine and analyze your class projects, assignments, and products for career development, you may want to explore more about the five categories that are used for that analysis.

The following sites, some of which offer a variety of assessment opportunities and link to other sites, will assist you in that exploration. We encourage you to explore many of the sites listed below.

*CRITICAL THINKING

Critical thinking assessment instruments were found on a variety of sites. Bloom's Taxonomy is included in this group as it is fundamental in the exploration of critical thinking.

> www.philosophy.unimelb.edu.au/reason/critical/
>
> www.sjsu.edu/depts/itl/
>
> www.calpress.com
>
> www.lgc.peachnet.edu/academic/educatn/Blooms/critical_thinking.htm

LEADERSHIP/INITIATIVE AND FOLLOW-THROUGH

We found that leadership and attributes such as initiative and follow-through often were linked in the assessment tools and literature.

> www.nsba.org/sbot/toolkit
>
> www.consultskills.com/
>
> www.luhc.org.uk/about/leaders/assessment.html
>
> www.vectorvisions.com/
>
> www.nwlink.com/~donclark/leader/self.html
>
> www.thefishergroup.com/tlea/
>
> http://ecs.engr.wisc.edu/student/selfassess.html

DIVERSITY

A search for cultural competence generated the links below that will allow you to explore working effectively with others and diversity.

> www.workforcedevelopmentgroup.com/individual_assess.html
>
> www.advocatesforyouth.org/publications/guide/chapter2.htm

COMMUNICATION

Communication style, on-line skills, organization, and presentation are explored in the sites listed here.

> http://sesweb.ses.pdx.edu/pdc/assessment/
>
> www.d.umn.edu/student/loon/acad/computer/comInternet.html

*If any of these links become broken, please check our website for periodic updates (www.prenhall.com/orton). We would also recommend that you familiarize yourself with resources available through the Prentice Hall supersite (www.prenhall.com/success).

www.goalminds.com/RateYou.cfm

http://saulcarliner.home.att.net/idbusiness/onlineassessment.htm

DEVELOPMENT SUGGESTIONS

Finally, after you get that first important job, continue to use your portfolio and the five categories to document and analyze your work tasks and assignments. Apply for your second job with a portfolio that demonstrates how you have successfully transitioned from student, to new work, to seasoned employee!

YOUR PORTFOLIO AND GRADUATE SCHOOL

Maturity begins when we're
content to feel right about
something without feeling
the necessity to prove
someone else wrong.

SYDNEY J. HARRIS

The process of applying to graduate school can also be intensive, challenging, and time consuming! Graduate schools can afford to be choosey with their admissions process. As you apply to graduate schools, we encourage you to think about the analysis of the undergraduate work you have already done while using this portfolio guide. You already have identified some of the key elements that graduate schools will be looking for:

- Critical thinking and problem solving
- Leadership
- Initiative and follow-through
- Working effectively with others/diversity
- Communication

The following are suggestions for integrating your portfolio development work into the graduate school application process.

- Edit and format your portfolio in a professional manner as you develop it.
- Make your targeted graduate school aware that you have a portfolio they can examine if you don't feel comfortable sending it unsolicited.
- Develop an abbreviated version of your portfolio that can be submitted along with your graduate school application. Include your personal statement, an overview of your achievements, and a description of key projects you have done that demonstrate the integration of the five categories. You should be able to draw those pieces directly from your portfolio.
- When you visit campuses, consider taking a complete copy of your portfolio to leave with admissions. This may be a greater investment than you can routinely afford but for those schools you feel strongly are a good fit, you may want to consider it an investment. The admissions advisor or chairperson may see it the same way.
- Graduate schools are interested in students who will go "above and beyond" the minimal requirements. Keep that in mind if you feel reluctant to submit your portfolio along with the graduate application.
- Include examples of your work in your portfolio. We suggest that you include not only the unmarked final drafts in your portfolio but also any work that demonstrates your development of a project, writing examples, collaboration skills, and use of processes

over time. This will help the graduate school advisor or chairperson estimate your abilities to integrate feedback, to learn, and to work as a team member.

■ Sometimes students are required to apply both to a graduate program and the particular school or department where they intend to study. Visit each office and consider leaving abbreviated or complete portfolios with both.